Building Character

Being Optimistic

by Penelope S. Nelson

Bullfrog Books

Ideas for Parents and Teachers

Bullfrog Books let children practice reading informational text at the earliest reading levels. Repetition, familiar words, and photo labels support early readers.

Before Reading

- Discuss the cover photo. What does it tell them?

- Look at the picture glossary together. Read and discuss the words.

Read the Book

- "Walk" through the book and look at the photos. Let the child ask questions. Point out the photo labels.

- Read the book to the child, or have him or her read independently.

After Reading

- Prompt the child to think more. Ask: Being optimistic can help us through difficult times. Can you think of a time when you stayed optimistic?

Bullfrog Books are published by Jump!
5357 Penn Avenue South
Minneapolis, MN 55419
www.jumplibrary.com

Library of Congress Cataloging-in-Publication Data

Names: Nelson, Penelope, 1994– author.
Title: Being optimistic / by Penelope S. Nelson.
Description: Minneapolis, MN: Jump!, Inc., [2020]
Series: Building character | Includes bibliographical references and index.
Identifiers: LCCN 2018050110 (print)
LCCN 2018057603 (ebook)
ISBN 9781641287135 (ebook)
ISBN 9781641287111 (hardcover: alk. paper)
ISBN 9781641287128 (paperback)
Subjects: LCSH: Optimism. | Cheerfulness.
Classification: LCC BF698.35.O57 (ebook) | LCC BF698.35.O57 N45 2020 (print) | DDC 149/.5—dc23
LC record available at https://lccn.loc.gov/2018050110

Editor: Jenna Trnka
Designer: Michelle Sonnek

Photo Credits: Samuel Borges Photography/ Shutterstock, cover; Syda Productions/ Shutterstock, 1; sirikorn thamniyom/Shutterstock, 3; PR Image Factory/Shutterstock, 4, 23tr; Sergey Novikov/Shutterstock, 5, 23bl; Lopolo/ Shutterstock, 6–7; somethingway/iStock, 8–9, 23br; wavebreakmedia/Shutterstock, 10–11; Veja/ Shutterstock, 12; LightField Studios/Shutterstock, 13; matooker/iStock, 14–15; Jacek Chabraszewski/ Shutterstock, 16; Hill Street Studios LLC/Getty, 17, 23tl; gostua/Shutterstock, 18–19; Darrin Henry/Shutterstock, 20–21; Roman Samokhin/ Shutterstock, 22 (card); FabrikaSimf/Shutterstock, 22 (markers); Ranta Images/Shutterstock, 24.

Printed in the United States of America at Corporate Graphics in North Mankato, Minnesota.

Table of Contents

Stay Positive

Let's be optimistic!

How?

We are positive.
We are hopeful!

Shae is new at school.
Will she make friends?
Yes!

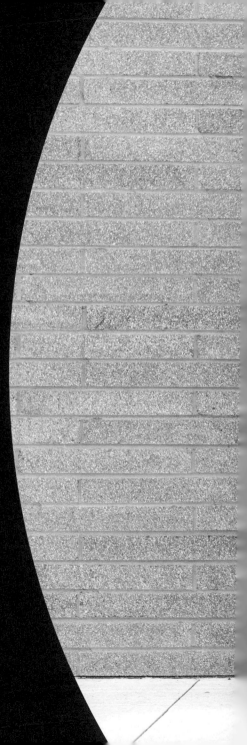

Max sings.

Good self-esteem helps.

He does well.

Nice job, Max!

Josh has a test.
Is he worried? No.
He studied.
He is ready!

Dom is scared.
Will he make the team?

Dad talks to him.

He helps him be hopeful.

Nice!

13

Gwen is up to bat.

She can do it!

bat

It is spelling bee day.

Jo's friends cheer for her.

Go, Jo!

She is confident!

Lou's dog is lost.

Lou does not get down.

He looks for her.

There is Luna!

Luna

Be hopeful!

You Can Do It!

How can you help others stay optimistic? Do you know someone who might need some encouragement? Is it a friend? A family member? Make that person a card! Write encouraging words inside. What are they good at? Tell them! Help them be positive. Remind them to stay optimistic!

Picture Glossary

confident
Having a strong belief
in your own abilities.

optimistic
Believing that things
will turn out well.

positive
Confident and enthusiastic.

self-esteem
A feeling of personal pride
and respect for yourself.

Index

To Learn More

Finding more information is as easy as 1, 2, 3.

❶ Go to www.factsurfer.com

❷ Enter "beingoptimistic" into the search box.

❸ Click the "Surf" button to see a list of websites.

24